50 Cooked and Cursed Recipes

By: Kelly Johnson

Table of Contents

- Haunted Herb-Crusted Chicken
- Spooky Smoky Blackened Ribs
- Witch's Brew Chili
- Cursed Cauldron Beef Stew
- Phantom Firecracker Shrimp
- Ghost Pepper Mac & Cheese
- Devil's Inferno Spicy Wings
- Bewitched BBQ Pulled Pork
- Hexed Honey-Glazed Carrots
- Voodoo Veggie Stir Fry
- Sorcerer's Spicy Sausage Pasta
- Banshee's Blood Red Velvet Cake
- Cursed Cauliflower Buffalo Bites
- Black Magic Mushroom Risotto
- Haunted Harvest Pumpkin Soup
- Spelltouched Sweet Potato Fries
- Phantom Pepperoni Pizza

- Wicked Whiskey Glazed Ribs
- Zombie Zesty Meatballs
- Shadow Steak Skewers
- Ghostly Garlic Bread
- Enchanted Eggplant Parmesan
- Hexed Herb Roasted Potatoes
- Poltergeist Pulled Chicken Sandwich
- Witch's Wicked Waffle Fries
- Haunted Honey BBQ Wings
- Spellbound Spaghetti Squash
- Cursed Cornbread Muffins
- Dark Magic Devil's Food Cake
- Phantom Pineapple Fried Rice
- Haunted Herb Butter Lobster
- Sorcerer's Sweet Chili Tofu
- Banshee's BBQ Bacon Bombs
- Blackout Black Bean Burgers
- Ghostly Garlic Shrimp Scampi
- Hexed Honey Mustard Glazed Ham

- Witch's Brew Vegetable Curry
- Cursed Cajun Catfish
- Shadowy Sweet & Sour Pork
- Phantom Pumpkin Spice Latte
- Haunted Herb-Crusted Salmon
- Bewitched Beef Bourguignon
- Spelltouched Sweet Corn Soup
- Dark Spell Double Chocolate Brownies
- Poltergeist Pesto Pasta
- Zombie Zesty Lime Chicken
- Wicked Wasabi Deviled Eggs
- Enchanted Egg Salad Sandwich
- Phantom Peach Cobbler
- Sorcerer's Spicy Szechuan Noodles

Haunted Herb-Crusted Chicken

Ingredients:

- 4 boneless, skinless chicken breasts
- 1/2 cup breadcrumbs
- 2 tbsp fresh parsley, chopped
- 1 tbsp fresh thyme, chopped
- 1 tbsp fresh rosemary, chopped
- 3 cloves garlic, minced
- 1/4 cup grated Parmesan cheese
- 1 tsp salt
- 1/2 tsp black pepper
- 2 tbsp olive oil
- 1 lemon, zested

Instructions:

1. Preheat oven to 400°F (200°C).
2. In a bowl, combine breadcrumbs, herbs, garlic, Parmesan, salt, pepper, and lemon zest.
3. Brush chicken breasts with olive oil, then press breadcrumb mixture onto each piece evenly.
4. Place chicken on a baking sheet lined with parchment paper.
5. Bake for 20-25 minutes, or until chicken is cooked through and crust is golden.

6. Serve with your choice of sides.

Spooky Smoky Blackened Ribs

Ingredients:

- 2 racks pork ribs
- 2 tbsp smoked paprika
- 1 tbsp garlic powder
- 1 tbsp onion powder
- 1 tbsp cayenne pepper
- 1 tbsp dried oregano
- 1 tbsp dried thyme
- 1 tsp black pepper
- 1 tsp salt
- 1/4 cup olive oil
- BBQ sauce, for glazing

Instructions:

1. Preheat oven to 300°F (150°C).
2. Mix all spices together in a bowl. Rub ribs with olive oil, then coat evenly with the spice mix.
3. Wrap ribs tightly in foil and place on a baking tray. Bake for 2.5 to 3 hours until tender.
4. Remove foil, brush ribs with BBQ sauce, and broil for 5-7 minutes until caramelized and smoky.

5. Slice and serve.

Witch's Brew Chili

Ingredients:

- 1 lb ground beef
- 1 onion, diced
- 3 cloves garlic, minced
- 1 bell pepper, diced
- 1 can (15 oz) kidney beans, drained and rinsed
- 1 can (15 oz) black beans, drained and rinsed
- 1 can (28 oz) crushed tomatoes
- 2 tbsp chili powder
- 1 tbsp cumin
- 1 tsp smoked paprika
- 1/2 tsp cayenne pepper
- Salt and pepper to taste
- 1 cup beef broth

Instructions:

1. In a large pot, brown ground beef over medium heat. Drain excess fat.
2. Add onion, garlic, and bell pepper; cook until softened.
3. Stir in chili powder, cumin, paprika, cayenne, salt, and pepper.
4. Add beans, crushed tomatoes, and beef broth.

5. Bring to a boil, then reduce heat and simmer for at least 45 minutes, stirring occasionally.

6. Serve with sour cream, shredded cheese, and chopped green onions.

Cursed Cauldron Beef Stew

Ingredients:

- 2 lbs beef stew meat, cubed
- 3 tbsp flour
- 3 tbsp olive oil
- 1 large onion, chopped
- 3 cloves garlic, minced
- 4 carrots, sliced
- 3 celery stalks, sliced
- 4 cups beef broth
- 1 cup red wine (optional)
- 2 bay leaves
- 1 tbsp fresh thyme
- Salt and pepper to taste
- 2 cups potatoes, cubed

Instructions:

1. Toss beef cubes with flour, salt, and pepper.
2. Heat olive oil in a large pot over medium-high heat. Brown beef on all sides, then remove.
3. Add onion and garlic to the pot; cook until softened.

4. Return beef to pot, add carrots, celery, potatoes, broth, wine, bay leaves, and thyme.

5. Bring to a simmer, cover, and cook for 2-3 hours until beef is tender.

6. Remove bay leaves before serving.

Phantom Firecracker Shrimp

Ingredients:

- 1 lb large shrimp, peeled and deveined
- 1/2 cup mayonnaise
- 2 tbsp sweet chili sauce
- 1 tbsp sriracha sauce
- 1 tsp lime juice
- 1/2 tsp garlic powder
- 1 cup panko breadcrumbs
- 2 eggs, beaten
- Oil for frying
- Green onions and sesame seeds for garnish

Instructions:

1. Mix mayonnaise, sweet chili sauce, sriracha, lime juice, and garlic powder in a bowl. Set aside.
2. Dip shrimp in beaten eggs, then coat with panko breadcrumbs.
3. Heat oil in a deep skillet to 350°F (175°C). Fry shrimp until golden and crispy, about 2-3 minutes. Drain on paper towels.
4. Toss fried shrimp in the spicy mayo sauce.
5. Garnish with sliced green onions and sesame seeds. Serve immediately.

Ghost Pepper Mac & Cheese

Ingredients:

- 8 oz elbow macaroni
- 3 tbsp butter
- 3 tbsp flour
- 3 cups milk
- 2 cups shredded sharp cheddar cheese
- 1 cup shredded mozzarella cheese
- 1/2 tsp ghost pepper powder (use sparingly!)
- Salt and pepper to taste
- 1/2 cup panko breadcrumbs

Instructions:

1. Cook macaroni according to package instructions. Drain and set aside.
2. In a saucepan, melt butter over medium heat. Stir in flour and cook 1 minute to form a roux.
3. Gradually whisk in milk, cooking until thickened.
4. Remove from heat, stir in cheeses until melted. Add ghost pepper powder carefully, salt, and pepper.
5. Combine cheese sauce with macaroni.
6. Transfer to a baking dish, sprinkle panko breadcrumbs on top.
7. Broil for 3-5 minutes until golden and bubbly. Serve hot.

Devil's Inferno Spicy Wings

Ingredients:

- 2 lbs chicken wings
- 1/2 cup hot sauce (like Frank's RedHot)
- 1/4 cup melted butter
- 1 tbsp cayenne pepper
- 1 tsp smoked paprika
- 1 tsp garlic powder
- Salt and pepper to taste
- Ranch or blue cheese dressing for serving

Instructions:

1. Preheat oven to 425°F (220°C).
2. Toss wings with salt, pepper, cayenne, paprika, and garlic powder. Spread on a baking sheet.
3. Bake wings for 40-45 minutes, flipping halfway through, until crispy and cooked through.
4. Mix hot sauce and melted butter. Toss baked wings in sauce until coated.
5. Serve with ranch or blue cheese dressing.

Bewitched BBQ Pulled Pork

Ingredients:

- 3-4 lb pork shoulder
- 2 tbsp smoked paprika
- 1 tbsp garlic powder
- 1 tbsp onion powder
- 1 tbsp brown sugar
- 1 tsp cayenne pepper
- Salt and pepper to taste
- 1 cup BBQ sauce
- 1/2 cup apple cider vinegar
- 1/2 cup water

Instructions:

1. Mix paprika, garlic powder, onion powder, brown sugar, cayenne, salt, and pepper. Rub all over pork shoulder.
2. Place pork in slow cooker with apple cider vinegar and water. Cook on low for 8 hours or until tender.
3. Shred pork with two forks and mix with BBQ sauce.
4. Serve on buns with coleslaw if desired.

Hexed Honey-Glazed Carrots

Ingredients:

- 1 lb baby carrots
- 2 tbsp butter
- 2 tbsp honey
- 1 tbsp brown sugar
- 1/2 tsp cinnamon
- 1/4 tsp salt
- 1/4 tsp black pepper

Instructions:

1. Boil carrots in salted water for 8–10 minutes until tender. Drain.
2. In a pan over medium heat, melt butter. Stir in honey, brown sugar, cinnamon, salt, and pepper.
3. Add carrots to the pan and toss to coat. Cook 3–5 minutes, stirring occasionally, until glazed.
4. Serve warm.

Voodoo Veggie Stir Fry
Ingredients:

- 1 tbsp sesame oil
- 1 cup broccoli florets
- 1 bell pepper, sliced
- 1 cup snap peas
- 1/2 red onion, sliced
- 2 cloves garlic, minced
- 1 tbsp soy sauce
- 1 tbsp hoisin sauce
- 1 tsp sriracha (optional)
- Sesame seeds for garnish

Instructions:

1. Heat sesame oil in a large skillet over medium-high heat.
2. Add garlic and onion, sauté for 2 minutes.
3. Add remaining vegetables and stir-fry for 5–7 minutes until just tender.
4. Stir in soy sauce, hoisin sauce, and sriracha. Cook another 1–2 minutes.
5. Garnish with sesame seeds and serve hot over rice or noodles.

Sorcerer's Spicy Sausage Pasta

Ingredients:

- 8 oz penne pasta
- 1/2 lb spicy Italian sausage, casings removed
- 1 tbsp olive oil
- 1/2 onion, diced
- 2 cloves garlic, minced
- 1/2 tsp red pepper flakes
- 1 can (15 oz) diced tomatoes
- 1/2 cup heavy cream
- Salt and pepper to taste
- Grated Parmesan and parsley for garnish

Instructions:

1. Cook pasta according to package directions. Drain and set aside.
2. In a skillet, heat olive oil over medium heat. Cook sausage until browned.
3. Add onion and garlic; sauté until translucent.
4. Stir in red pepper flakes and tomatoes. Simmer 10 minutes.
5. Add cream, salt, and pepper. Simmer 2 more minutes.
6. Combine with cooked pasta. Top with Parmesan and parsley.

Banshee's Blood Red Velvet Cake

Ingredients:

- 2 1/2 cups flour
- 1 1/2 cups sugar
- 1 tsp baking soda
- 1 tsp cocoa powder
- 1/2 tsp salt
- 1 1/2 cups vegetable oil
- 1 cup buttermilk
- 2 large eggs
- 2 tbsp red food coloring
- 1 tsp vanilla extract
- 1 tsp white vinegar

Instructions:

1. Preheat oven to 350°F (175°C). Grease two 9-inch round cake pans.
2. In a bowl, whisk dry ingredients together.
3. In another bowl, mix oil, buttermilk, eggs, food coloring, vanilla, and vinegar.
4. Combine wet and dry ingredients until smooth.
5. Divide batter between pans. Bake 30–35 minutes.
6. Cool completely before frosting with cream cheese frosting.

Cursed Cauliflower Buffalo Bites

Ingredients:

- 1 head cauliflower, cut into florets
- 1/2 cup flour
- 1/2 cup water
- 1 tsp garlic powder
- 1/4 tsp salt
- 1/4 tsp pepper
- 1/2 cup buffalo sauce
- 1 tbsp melted butter

Instructions:

1. Preheat oven to 425°F (220°C).
2. Mix flour, water, garlic powder, salt, and pepper into a smooth batter.
3. Dip cauliflower florets into batter and place on a lined baking sheet.
4. Bake 20 minutes, flipping halfway.
5. Mix buffalo sauce and butter. Toss baked cauliflower in sauce.
6. Return to oven for 10 more minutes. Serve with ranch or blue cheese.

Black Magic Mushroom Risotto

Ingredients:

- 1 tbsp olive oil
- 1 small onion, finely chopped
- 2 cloves garlic, minced
- 1 1/2 cups arborio rice
- 1/2 cup dry white wine
- 4 cups warm vegetable broth
- 1 1/2 cups mushrooms, sliced
- 1/4 cup grated Parmesan
- Salt and pepper to taste
- Fresh thyme for garnish

Instructions:

1. Heat olive oil in a saucepan. Cook onion and garlic until translucent.
2. Add rice, stir for 2 minutes.
3. Pour in wine; stir until absorbed.
4. Add broth 1/2 cup at a time, stirring constantly and letting it absorb before adding more.
5. Sauté mushrooms separately, then add to rice halfway through.
6. When rice is tender and creamy, stir in Parmesan, salt, and pepper.

7. Garnish with thyme.

Haunted Harvest Pumpkin Soup

Ingredients:

- 2 tbsp butter
- 1 onion, chopped
- 2 cloves garlic, minced
- 1 can (15 oz) pumpkin purée
- 2 cups vegetable broth
- 1/2 cup heavy cream or coconut milk
- 1/2 tsp nutmeg
- Salt and pepper to taste
- Pumpkin seeds and sour cream for garnish

Instructions:

1. Melt butter in a pot over medium heat. Cook onion and garlic until soft.
2. Stir in pumpkin, broth, and nutmeg. Bring to a simmer for 10 minutes.
3. Blend until smooth. Stir in cream, salt, and pepper.
4. Heat through and serve with pumpkin seeds and sour cream on top.

Spelltouched Sweet Potato Fries

Ingredients:

- 2 large sweet potatoes, cut into fries
- 2 tbsp olive oil
- 1 tsp smoked paprika
- 1/2 tsp garlic powder
- 1/2 tsp cayenne pepper
- Salt and pepper to taste

Instructions:

1. Preheat oven to 425°F (220°C).
2. Toss sweet potato fries with olive oil and spices.
3. Spread in a single layer on a baking sheet.
4. Bake for 25–30 minutes, flipping halfway, until crispy.
5. Serve hot with your favorite dipping sauce.

Phantom Pepperoni Pizza

Ingredients:

- 1 pizza dough (store-bought or homemade)
- 1/2 cup pizza sauce
- 1 1/2 cups shredded mozzarella
- 20 pepperoni slices
- 1 tsp Italian seasoning
- Olive oil for brushing

Instructions:

1. Preheat oven to 475°F (245°C).
2. Roll out dough on a floured surface and place on a baking sheet or pizza stone.
3. Spread sauce evenly, top with cheese, pepperoni, and seasoning.
4. Lightly brush crust with olive oil.
5. Bake for 12–15 minutes until crust is golden and cheese is bubbling.
6. Slice and serve hot.

Wicked Whiskey Glazed Ribs

Ingredients:

- 2 racks baby back ribs
- Salt and pepper
- 1 cup whiskey
- 1 cup ketchup
- 1/2 cup brown sugar
- 2 tbsp apple cider vinegar
- 2 cloves garlic, minced
- 1 tsp smoked paprika

Instructions:

1. Season ribs with salt and pepper. Wrap in foil and bake at 300°F (150°C) for 2.5 hours.
2. In a saucepan, combine whiskey, ketchup, sugar, vinegar, garlic, and paprika. Simmer until thickened (15–20 minutes).
3. Unwrap ribs, brush with glaze, and broil or grill for 5–10 minutes until caramelized.
4. Slice and serve.

Zombie Zesty Meatballs

Ingredients:

- 1 lb ground beef
- 1/2 cup breadcrumbs
- 1/4 cup grated Parmesan
- 1 egg
- 2 cloves garlic, minced
- 1 tsp Italian seasoning
- Salt and pepper
- 2 cups marinara sauce

Instructions:

1. Mix beef, breadcrumbs, cheese, egg, garlic, and seasoning. Shape into balls.
2. Brown meatballs in a skillet over medium heat.
3. Add marinara sauce, cover, and simmer 20 minutes.
4. Serve with pasta or toothpicks as creepy cocktail bites.

Shadow Steak Skewers

Ingredients:

- 1 lb sirloin steak, cubed
- 2 tbsp olive oil
- 2 tbsp soy sauce
- 1 tbsp Worcestershire sauce
- 1 tsp garlic powder
- 1 tsp smoked paprika
- Skewers, soaked if wooden

Instructions:

1. Marinate steak cubes in oil, soy sauce, Worcestershire, and spices for 30 minutes.
2. Thread onto skewers.
3. Grill or broil for 8–10 minutes, turning once, until desired doneness.
4. Serve with spooky dipping sauce.

Ghostly Garlic Bread

Ingredients:

- 1 baguette, sliced lengthwise
- 1/2 cup butter, softened
- 3 cloves garlic, minced
- 2 tbsp chopped parsley
- 1/4 tsp salt
- 1/2 cup shredded mozzarella (optional)

Instructions:

1. Mix butter, garlic, parsley, and salt.
2. Spread on baguette halves. Top with cheese if desired.
3. Bake at 375°F (190°C) for 10–12 minutes until golden.
4. Slice and serve warm.

Enchanted Eggplant Parmesan

Ingredients:

- 2 eggplants, sliced into rounds
- 1 tsp salt
- 1 cup flour
- 2 eggs, beaten
- 1 1/2 cups breadcrumbs
- 2 cups marinara sauce
- 2 cups shredded mozzarella
- 1/2 cup grated Parmesan

Instructions:

1. Salt eggplant slices and let sit 30 minutes. Pat dry.
2. Dredge in flour, dip in egg, coat in breadcrumbs.
3. Bake at 400°F (200°C) for 20 minutes, flipping once.
4. In a baking dish, layer sauce, eggplant, mozzarella, and Parmesan. Repeat.
5. Bake 25 minutes until bubbly. Let rest before serving.

Hexed Herb Roasted Potatoes

Ingredients:

- 2 lbs baby potatoes, halved
- 2 tbsp olive oil
- 1 tsp rosemary
- 1 tsp thyme
- 1 tsp garlic powder
- Salt and pepper to taste

Instructions:

1. Preheat oven to 425°F (220°C).
2. Toss potatoes with oil and herbs.
3. Spread on a baking sheet in a single layer.
4. Roast for 30–35 minutes, turning once, until golden and crispy.
5. Serve hot and hexed.

Poltergeist Pulled Chicken Sandwich

Ingredients:

- 2 boneless chicken breasts
- 1 cup BBQ sauce
- 1/2 cup chicken broth
- 1 tbsp brown sugar
- 1 tsp smoked paprika
- Burger buns

Instructions:

1. Place chicken, BBQ sauce, broth, sugar, and paprika in a slow cooker.
2. Cook on low 6 hours or high 3 hours.
3. Shred chicken and return to sauce.
4. Serve on buns with slaw or pickles.

Witch's Wicked Waffle Fries

Ingredients:

- 1 bag frozen waffle fries
- 1/2 tsp garlic powder
- 1/2 tsp smoked paprika
- Salt to taste
- 1/4 cup shredded cheddar (optional)
- Fresh parsley for garnish

Instructions:

1. Cook fries according to package instructions until crispy.
2. Toss with garlic powder, paprika, and salt.
3. Top with cheddar (if using) and bake an additional 2 minutes to melt.
4. Garnish with parsley and serve hot.

Haunted Honey BBQ Wings

Ingredients:

- 2 lbs chicken wings
- Salt and pepper
- 1/2 cup BBQ sauce
- 1/4 cup honey
- 1 tbsp hot sauce (optional)

Instructions:

1. Preheat oven to 400°F (200°C).
2. Season wings with salt and pepper. Bake on a rack-lined tray for 40–45 minutes.
3. In a bowl, mix BBQ sauce, honey, and hot sauce.
4. Toss wings in sauce and return to oven for 10 more minutes.
5. Serve sticky and spooky.

Spellbound Spaghetti Squash

Ingredients:

- 1 medium spaghetti squash
- 2 tbsp olive oil
- Salt and pepper
- 1/2 cup marinara sauce
- 1/4 cup grated Parmesan
- 1 tsp Italian seasoning

Instructions:

1. Halve squash, remove seeds, drizzle with oil, season, and bake at 400°F (200°C) for 40 minutes.
2. Scrape with a fork to create strands.
3. Toss with marinara, Parmesan, and seasoning.
4. Serve in squash shell or a bowl.

Cursed Cornbread Muffins
Ingredients:

- 1 cup cornmeal
- 1 cup flour
- 1/4 cup sugar
- 1 tbsp baking powder
- 1/2 tsp salt
- 1 cup milk
- 1/4 cup melted butter
- 2 eggs

Instructions:

1. Preheat oven to 375°F (190°C).
2. Mix dry ingredients in one bowl, wet in another.
3. Combine and pour into muffin tin.
4. Bake for 15–18 minutes until golden.
5. Cool slightly before serving.

Dark Magic Devil's Food Cake
Ingredients:

- 1 3/4 cups flour
- 3/4 cup cocoa powder
- 1 1/2 tsp baking powder
- 1 1/2 tsp baking soda
- 1/2 tsp salt
- 2 eggs
- 1 cup buttermilk
- 1/2 cup vegetable oil
- 1 tsp vanilla extract
- 1 cup boiling water
- 1 3/4 cups sugar

Instructions:

1. Preheat oven to 350°F (175°C). Grease two cake pans.
2. Mix dry ingredients. In another bowl, whisk eggs, buttermilk, oil, vanilla.
3. Combine, then slowly mix in boiling water.
4. Pour into pans and bake 30–35 minutes.
5. Cool and frost with dark chocolate icing.

Phantom Pineapple Fried Rice

Ingredients:

- 2 cups cooked rice (cold)
- 1 cup pineapple chunks
- 1/2 cup diced carrots
- 1/2 cup peas
- 2 eggs, scrambled
- 2 tbsp soy sauce
- 1 tbsp sesame oil
- 2 green onions, sliced

Instructions:

1. Heat oil in skillet or wok. Sauté carrots and peas.
2. Add rice and stir-fry 3 minutes.
3. Add eggs, soy sauce, pineapple, and green onions.
4. Cook another 2–3 minutes. Serve hot.

Haunted Herb Butter Lobster

Ingredients:

- 2 lobster tails
- 1/4 cup melted butter
- 1 tsp garlic, minced
- 1 tsp parsley
- 1/2 tsp thyme
- Lemon wedges

Instructions:

1. Preheat oven to broil.
2. Split lobster tails, brush with herb butter mixture.
3. Broil for 8–10 minutes until opaque and slightly browned.
4. Serve with lemon wedges and extra butter.

Sorcerer's Sweet Chili Tofu
Ingredients:

- 1 block extra-firm tofu, cubed
- 1 tbsp cornstarch
- 2 tbsp oil
- 1/3 cup sweet chili sauce
- 1 tbsp soy sauce
- 1 tsp sesame seeds
- Chopped scallions

Instructions:

1. Toss tofu in cornstarch. Fry in oil until golden on all sides.
2. In a bowl, mix chili sauce and soy sauce.
3. Toss tofu in sauce.
4. Garnish with sesame seeds and scallions. Serve over rice or noodles.

Banshee's BBQ Bacon Bombs

Ingredients:

- 1 lb ground beef
- 1/2 cup shredded cheddar cheese
- 1/4 cup diced onions
- 8 slices bacon
- 1/2 cup BBQ sauce

Instructions:

1. Preheat oven to 400°F (200°C).
2. Mix ground beef, cheese, and onions. Form into 4 balls.
3. Wrap each with 2 slices of bacon.
4. Place on baking sheet and brush with BBQ sauce.
5. Bake 25–30 minutes. Brush with more sauce before serving.

Blackout Black Bean Burgers

Ingredients:

- 1 (15 oz) can black beans, drained and mashed
- 1/2 cup breadcrumbs
- 1/4 cup finely diced red onion
- 1 clove garlic, minced
- 1 egg
- 1 tsp cumin
- Salt and pepper to taste

Instructions:

1. Combine all ingredients and form into 4 patties.
2. Chill 20 minutes.
3. Cook in a skillet over medium heat 4–5 minutes per side.
4. Serve on buns with your favorite toppings.

Ghostly Garlic Shrimp Scampi

Ingredients:

- 1 lb shrimp, peeled and deveined
- 3 tbsp butter
- 4 cloves garlic, minced
- 1/4 tsp red pepper flakes
- Juice of 1 lemon
- 1/4 cup chopped parsley
- Salt and pepper to taste
- 8 oz spaghetti or linguine

Instructions:

1. Cook pasta and set aside.
2. In a skillet, melt butter. Add garlic and red pepper flakes.
3. Add shrimp, cook 2–3 minutes per side.
4. Add lemon juice, parsley, salt, and pepper.
5. Toss with pasta and serve.

Hexed Honey Mustard Glazed Ham
Ingredients:

- 1 (3–4 lb) boneless ham
- 1/4 cup honey
- 1/4 cup Dijon mustard
- 2 tbsp brown sugar
- 1 tbsp apple cider vinegar

Instructions:

1. Preheat oven to 350°F (175°C).
2. Mix glaze ingredients and brush over ham.
3. Bake for 1–1.5 hours, brushing with glaze every 20 minutes.
4. Rest 10 minutes before slicing.

Witch's Brew Vegetable Curry

Ingredients:

- 1 tbsp oil
- 1 onion, chopped
- 2 cloves garlic, minced
- 1 tbsp curry powder
- 1 tsp turmeric
- 2 cups mixed vegetables (carrots, peas, potatoes)
- 1 can coconut milk
- Salt to taste
- Fresh cilantro

Instructions:

1. Sauté onion and garlic in oil until soft.
2. Add curry powder and turmeric; cook 1 minute.
3. Add vegetables and coconut milk. Simmer until tender.
4. Season with salt and garnish with cilantro. Serve with rice.

Cursed Cajun Catfish

Ingredients:

- 2 catfish fillets
- 1 tbsp Cajun seasoning
- 1 tbsp olive oil
- Lemon wedges

Instructions:

1. Rub fillets with Cajun seasoning.
2. Heat oil in skillet over medium-high heat.
3. Cook fillets 3–4 minutes per side.
4. Serve with lemon wedges.

Shadowy Sweet & Sour Pork

Ingredients:

- 1 lb pork loin, cubed
- 1/2 cup cornstarch
- 1/4 cup vegetable oil
- 1/2 cup diced bell peppers
- 1/2 cup pineapple chunks
- 1/4 cup vinegar
- 1/4 cup ketchup
- 1/4 cup sugar
- 1 tbsp soy sauce

Instructions:

1. Coat pork in cornstarch. Fry in oil until crispy.
2. Remove pork. In same pan, cook peppers and pineapple.
3. Add vinegar, ketchup, sugar, and soy sauce. Simmer 5 minutes.
4. Return pork to pan and toss to coat. Serve with rice.

Phantom Pumpkin Spice Latte
 Ingredients:

- 1 cup milk
- 1/4 cup brewed espresso or strong coffee
- 2 tbsp pumpkin purée
- 1 tbsp sugar
- 1/4 tsp pumpkin pie spice
- Whipped cream (optional)

Instructions:

1. In a small pot, whisk milk, pumpkin, sugar, and spice until warm.
2. Stir in coffee.
3. Pour into a mug and top with whipped cream if desired.

Haunted Herb-Crusted Salmon

Ingredients:

- 2 salmon fillets
- 1 tbsp olive oil
- 1 tbsp chopped fresh herbs (parsley, dill, thyme)
- Salt and pepper
- Lemon wedges

Instructions:

1. Preheat oven to 375°F (190°C).
2. Place salmon on baking sheet, brush with oil, season, and press herbs on top.
3. Bake 12–15 minutes. Serve with lemon wedges.

Bewitched Beef Bourguignon

Ingredients:

- 2 lbs beef chuck, cut into 2-inch cubes
- Salt & black pepper
- 2 tbsp flour
- 4 strips bacon, chopped
- 1 large onion, diced
- 3 cloves garlic, minced
- 2 cups red wine
- 2 cups beef broth
- 2 tbsp tomato paste
- 1 tsp thyme
- 2 bay leaves
- 1 lb carrots, sliced
- 1/2 lb pearl onions
- 1/2 lb mushrooms, halved
- 2 tbsp butter

Instructions:

1. Preheat oven to 325°F (160°C).
2. Season beef with salt and pepper, then dust with flour.

3. In a Dutch oven, cook bacon until crisp; remove.

4. Brown beef in bacon fat in batches. Remove.

5. Sauté onions and garlic until softened.

6. Add wine, broth, tomato paste, thyme, bay leaves. Bring to boil.

7. Return beef and bacon to pot. Cover and bake for 2 hours.

8. Sauté carrots, mushrooms, and pearl onions in butter. Add to pot.

9. Bake uncovered 30 minutes more. Serve hot.

Spelltouched Sweet Corn Soup

Ingredients:

- 4 ears of fresh corn or 3 cups frozen corn
- 1 tbsp butter
- 1 small onion, chopped
- 1 garlic clove, minced
- 2 cups vegetable or chicken broth
- 1/2 cup heavy cream
- Salt and pepper to taste
- Chopped chives (optional)

Instructions:

1. In a pot, melt butter. Sauté onion and garlic until translucent.
2. Add corn and cook 5 minutes.
3. Add broth, simmer 15 minutes.
4. Blend soup until smooth, return to pot.
5. Stir in cream, season with salt and pepper.
6. Simmer 5 more minutes. Garnish with chives if desired.

Dark Spell Double Chocolate Brownies

Ingredients:

- 1/2 cup unsalted butter
- 1 cup sugar
- 2 large eggs
- 1 tsp vanilla extract
- 1/3 cup unsweetened cocoa powder
- 1/2 cup all-purpose flour
- 1/4 tsp salt
- 1/4 tsp baking powder
- 1/2 cup semi-sweet chocolate chips

Instructions:

1. Preheat oven to 350°F (175°C). Grease an 8x8-inch baking pan.
2. Melt butter. Stir in sugar, eggs, and vanilla.
3. Add cocoa, flour, salt, and baking powder. Mix until combined.
4. Fold in chocolate chips.
5. Pour into pan. Bake 20–25 minutes. Cool before slicing.

Poltergeist Pesto Pasta

Ingredients:

- 12 oz pasta (penne or spaghetti)
- 2 cups fresh basil leaves
- 1/3 cup pine nuts
- 2 garlic cloves
- 1/2 cup grated Parmesan cheese
- 1/2 cup olive oil
- Salt and pepper to taste

Instructions:

1. Cook pasta according to package. Drain and set aside.
2. In a food processor, blend basil, pine nuts, garlic, and Parmesan.
3. Slowly stream in olive oil until smooth.
4. Toss pesto with pasta. Season with salt and pepper. Serve warm or chilled.

Zombie Zesty Lime Chicken

Ingredients:

- 4 boneless chicken breasts
- 1/4 cup olive oil
- Juice of 2 limes
- Zest of 1 lime
- 2 cloves garlic, minced
- 1 tsp cumin
- Salt and pepper to taste

Instructions:

1. Combine oil, lime juice/zest, garlic, cumin, salt, and pepper.
2. Marinate chicken in mixture for at least 30 minutes.
3. Grill or pan-sear chicken 6–7 minutes per side or until cooked through.
4. Serve with lime wedges.

Wicked Wasabi Deviled Eggs

Ingredients:

- 6 hard-boiled eggs
- 3 tbsp mayonnaise
- 1 tsp wasabi paste (adjust to taste)
- 1/2 tsp rice vinegar
- Salt to taste
- Chopped green onion for garnish

Instructions:

1. Halve eggs, remove yolks.
2. Mash yolks with mayo, wasabi, vinegar, and salt.
3. Spoon or pipe mixture into egg whites.
4. Garnish with green onion.

Enchanted Egg Salad Sandwich

Ingredients:

- 6 hard-boiled eggs, chopped
- 1/4 cup mayonnaise
- 1 tsp Dijon mustard
- 1 tbsp chopped dill or chives
- Salt and pepper to taste
- Bread or rolls of choice

Instructions:

1. Mix eggs, mayo, mustard, herbs, salt, and pepper.
2. Chill 15 minutes.
3. Serve on bread or rolls with lettuce if desired.

Phantom Peach Cobbler

Ingredients:

- 4 cups sliced peaches (fresh or canned)
- 1/2 cup sugar
- 1 tsp cinnamon
- 1 cup flour
- 1 cup milk
- 1/2 cup butter, melted
- 1 tbsp baking powder
- 1/4 tsp salt

Instructions:

1. Preheat oven to 350°F (175°C).
2. In a baking dish, pour melted butter.
3. In bowl, mix flour, milk, sugar, baking powder, and salt. Pour over butter—do not stir.
4. Top with peaches and cinnamon.
5. Bake 40–45 minutes until golden and bubbly.

Sorcerer's Spicy Szechuan Noodles

Ingredients:

- 8 oz noodles (lo mein or spaghetti)
- 2 tbsp soy sauce
- 1 tbsp rice vinegar
- 1 tbsp Szechuan chili oil or sauce
- 1 tsp sesame oil
- 1 garlic clove, minced
- 1/2 tsp sugar
- 2 green onions, sliced
- Optional: crushed peanuts or sesame seeds

Instructions:

1. Cook noodles, drain, and rinse with cold water.
2. In a bowl, whisk sauces, oils, garlic, and sugar.
3. Toss noodles in sauce.
4. Garnish with green onions and optional toppings.

www.ingramcontent.com/pod-product-compliance
Lightning Source LLC
LaVergne TN
LVHW081319060526
838201LV00055B/2365